WRESTLING WITH GOD

SAINT JOHN'S UNIVERSITY PRESS

COLLEGEVILLE, MINNESOTA

Kilian McDonnell, OSB

[signature: Kilian McDonnell, OSB]

WRESTLING
WITH
GOD

Cover design: Alan Reed, OSB. Photo courtesy of
Thinkstock and Istockphoto.com.
Interior design: David Manahan, OSB.
Editor: Julie Walnum.

Scripture texts in this work are taken from the *New
Revised Standard Version Bible* © 1989, Division of
Christian Education of the National Council of the
Churches of Christ in the United States of America.
Used by permission. All rights reserved.

Library of Congress Cataloging-in-Publication Data

McDonnell, Kilian.
    Wrestling with God / Kilian McDonnell.
        p.   cm.
    Includes bibliographical references.
    ISBN 978-0-9740992-8-6
    1. Christian poetry, American.   I. Title.
PS3613.C3878W74   2011
811'.6—dc22   2011016459

To the monks
of the international Holy Trinity Monastery,
Fujimi, Japan,
whose monks witness to the Gospel
through community life,
work, and prayer for world peace.
The monastery constitutes a center
of hospitality, learning, and culture.

CONTENTS

COUNT THREE

AUTHOR'S NOTE

My model for these biblical poems is Jacob wrestling with
one whom he at first thinks is a man but later realizes is
God. When Jacob is winning, the Lord puts Jacob's hip out
of socket, thus cheating. Jacob has an arm hold on God as
they wrestle through the night. At dawn God asks Jacob
to let him go, but Jacob will agree only if God blesses him
and tells him what God's name is. God refuses to divulge
the name but does bless Jacob who walks away limping
(Gen 32:23-32).

    Generally I set aside sacral language that may reflect
the mind of the sacred author of the biblical text but not
the speech of the biblical characters themselves. Instead I
use the idiom of the common people. The earthy language
is borrowed from Old Testament texts.

STEPPING INTO THE RING

IN THE BEGINNING

*In the beginning when God created the heavens and the
earth, the earth was a formless void and darkness covered
the face of the deep. Genesis 1:1-2*

Out there, no space,
no up or down, no time,
no color, no meaning;

nothing. Since I created time
I want to share my God-self,
fill the void with mirrors

of my face: suns, Mount Fuji,
Nelly the cow, bananas
and black beetles. I dig in the dirt,

sculpt jeweled icons of myself,
bend down to breathe astonishment
into nostrils male and female,

me writ small—and under
their feet I place things living:
worms, elephants with floppy ears,

horse mango trees that bear orange fruit
at 300 years. To Adam and Eve
I give quarrelling Cain and Abel,

and hunger for the future
paradise. By day seven
my fingernails are broken

from digging in the dirt.
Anyway I'm tired so I Sabbath,
leave creation unfinished.

DOUBT HAS REASONS

A great windstorm arose, and the waves beat into the boat,
so that the boat was already being swamped. Mark 4:37

This is ridiculous.
An enraged dragon
at the bottom of the sea
empties out the guts of Hell,
winds whip us to despair,
clouds drop chaos,
the sea breaks above our heads,
water to our ankles,
we are going down
and you sleep on the prow,
your head upon a pillow.

THE CALL

As he walked by the Sea of Galilee, he saw two brothers, . . .
Peter, and Andrew. Matthew 4:18

Some of us were village fishermen,
unripe grapes on a bruised stem, wise
in the deep waters' moods and treacheries,
    when we heard the call.

In the boat we sat
for hours reading the meaning
of the clouds, the movement
    of the waters, and dreamt

of catching nets full
to breaking of sprat hiding
in the caverns of the deep.
    The fishing done and on the beach,

we bent to weigh the catch,
undo snarled ropes, patch tears
—silent except for snatches of man talk
    and what the morrow will bring.

What hidden unmeasured force
in the naked "Come follow me!"
the stranger walking past us
    uttered but once,

unexpected as a starboard gust of wind.
Abandon boat, teenage children, pregnant wives,
to go into the threat of the unknown?
    We rose to follow.

HAMMER, SPIKE, MARY

On the third day there was a wedding in Cana of Galilee, and the
mother of Jesus was there. John 2:1

I remember the pain days like the time
I told my son, *The wine jug's empty,*
and he replied, *Neither your business nor mine.*
I felt he'd hammered a spike
into the breasts he'd cried for and sucked.

My son built a rampart against me
as though I were a Philistine.
Example: he refused to see his kin and me
though he knew we'd walked the thirty miles
from Nazareth. He was busy seeing strangers.

Not a single member of his family
among the men he'd chosen to walk
with him. As though we'd quarreled,
my son moved out of home,
out of Nazareth to live in Peter's house

in lovely seashore Capernaum twenty miles
from me and family. Other women traveled with him
as he preached, exorcised, and healed. For thirteen men
they found free lodging, prepared meals of bread,
goat cheese, date juice, and dried locusts moistened

with vinegar. So where was I?
Alone in Nazareth sewing patches on my skirt
while women whispered. He distanced himself
as though I'd disgraced myself with the fish monger.
For a man of thirty this cannot be adolescent rebellion.

COSMOS AND ROCK

But on the first day of the week, at early dawn, they came to the tomb. Luke 24:1

He died an ambitious death.
Young in his dying as though
he could not wait. A fool
to his family who thought
He wasted life

like sowing wheat on parched soil.
His blood had seeped
onto the linen bands
and clotted to a stiffness
like wet towels drying

in the freezing wind. After three
days his arms move
beneath the winding bands
as though eternity protests lolling
abed. No need of an opening

to the light as his body shines
like the burning Sinai bush.
He sits up, takes the napkin
from his forehead, folds it
as one does after mutton soup,

places it upon the ledge behind him.
As he rises through the stone
the cosmos lurches.

Voices of women wondering
who will roll away the rock for them.

PETER'S WIFE CLIMBS INTO BED

*I tell you, you are Peter, and on this rock I will build my
church. Matthew 16:18*

Betrayals?
A wife understands no love
escapes subversions.
Rocks have surface grit, pits,
blotches. I know my Peter's chinks,
know rocks can crack.

When Peter draws me toward him
I feel my apostolic lover's fingers
upon my breasts. I pull the beard
that scratches when we lie together
and we tell each other who we are.

I share his joy in master's choice.
My beloved goes preaching
terrible mysteries
while I pine for pillow talk.
When he returns

we'll climb in bed,
he'll draw me toward him
while I pull his beard,
whisper in his ear,
I'm pregnant.

ADJUSTABLE CONSCIENCES

The chief priests and the scribes were looking for a way to put Jesus to death, for they were afraid of the people. Luke 22:2

Nasty business this betrayal.
Even manageably pure priestly motives
need to shroud the necessary sin

in sacred silk; bought blood
poured upon the altar
still stinks. But he makes himself

the Sabbath's Lord, deconstructs the temple
stone by stone, torches the Pentateuch,
thrusts a spear into Israel's gut,

and we die. His blood or ours?
Some events push priests
to adjust pure consciences

to sacred needs. In any case,
we follow Leviticus:
blood for blood.

Thirty pieces of silver
could not be better spent.

JUDAS BETWEEN LOVE AND BETRAYAL

Of those you have given me I have not lost one.
John 6:39, 17:12

When I close the door behind me
the hinges squeak as the light
is blotted out and wood against

wood makes a thud of finality.
I weep as I walk the street
toward the temple gate.

Still it must be done:
beat ploughshares into swords
to drive the Romans out.

Betrayal pours damnation
in my wine. Why
does his love have a fence?

BY THE WAVE
OF THE MAGICIAN'S WAND

*Our chief priests and leaders handed him over to be
condemned to death and crucified him. But we had hoped
that he was the one to redeem Israel. Luke 24:20-21*

I'm Peter, the Rock,
on whom our Jesus built his church.
He told me to steady the unsteady
but now this boulder wobbles
and wonders.
When he gasped and died
the universe collapsed
into a sinkhole.

We fishermen,
who gave up fishing
at his command,
will not sit
on teakwood thrones,
wear royal rings
set with lapis lazuli;
no one will prostrate
before us.

Was it all dazzle
we believed?
Was walking on the water
illusion? Was it
with the wave
of the magician's wand
he pulled bread and fish
from the basket?
In a word,
did the good news
become bad?

I'm going fishing.

A SECOND BETRAYAL

One of the thieves was saved, do not despair; one of the thieves was damned, do not presume. St. Augustine

Augustine, my friend, you got it almost right.
Dismas went to be with Jesus
the very day he died because Jesus
turned his head slightly to avoid seeing him

snatch the temple's gold menorah.
You believe the other thief who did the same
went to hell. I wonder.
Some crooks choose Hades,

but we do not know of any person there.
We're not even sure Judas went down,
he who was elected to see
what the eye cannot see, to hear

what the ear cannot hear, to understand
what the heart cannot imagine.
And his betrayal was double.
When Judas pushed aside God's

mercy hand, he pushed away forgiveness.
Is this not a second betrayal—and this just
before he hangs the rope upon the tree?
But, Augustine, my friend,

who are we to say Judas did not,
in that last instant, as the rope was strangling life,
and darkness had not descended,
grip God's little finger?

PETER CONFESSES TO JUDAS

When Judas, his betrayer, saw that Jesus was condemned,
he repented and brought back the thirty pieces of silver.
Matthew 27:3

From the first he chose you.
You saw him feed five thousand
with five loaves of bread and two fish.
You saw him walk upon the sea.

You were there when Jesus
shouted Lazarus's name
and he waddled from the tomb.

Death was just an inconvenience.

We all fled into the night
like doves frightened by a hawk.
We were all traitors,
letting him die that stupid death.

Who has the greater sin?

You betrayed him once for silver coins
to buy bronze-tipped arrows
to drive the Romans out.

I betrayed him three times for nothing.

HIS BRAIN LEAKS

*Then he [Jesus] went home [to Capernaum]; and the crowd
came together again, so that they could not even eat. When
his family [in Nazareth] heard it, they went out to restrain
him, for people were saying, "He has gone out of his mind."*
Mark 3:20-21

One day he's sawing cypress planks
in Nazareth, the next
he's in Capernaum
teaching against temple and Torah.

Rumor has it he's running
around dropping miracles
as though he were a god
who'd sprung a leak in his brain.

Around him the sick seeking cures
for their rickety children.
Some plead to have shrieking demons
sent back to hell, while others want
another Moses who will raise his arms,
part waters, and drown Caesar's legions.

Cousin Jesus has no time
to eat a crust of bread.

Six of us are off
to Capernaum to bring him home.
I have the rope,
Joses the gag,
and Mary leads the donkey.

Peter's house
where he lives
is blocked by worthies and crazies.
We cannot get in and he will not come out
to greet his mother
who walked the twenty miles.

Says his family's inside.

TABLE TALK

While they were eating, he took a loaf of bread . . . and
said, "Take; this is my body." . . . Then he took a cup. . . .
He said, "This is my blood." Mark 14:22-24

A donkey brays in the street below
while Magdalene ascends the creaky stairs
carrying a platter of flatbread
she just pulled from the clay
street-oven. Bending down
(wrist bangles jangling)
she lays her bread before the Master
and the twelve of us reclining
on grey reed mats and brocaded pillows.

Rachel leans over those at table
and with a thud sets down
a red-glazed crock
full of cheap red wine
that tastes like cheap red wine.

Peter lays back and whispers to John
as Rabbi Jesus rises,
shifts his prayer shawl
—the chatter stops.

He intones Hallel Psalm 113,
says the bread and wine *are* him
and something about death and memory.

Dogs bark in the distance.

No one understands
but, like the feigning deaf,
we nod "got it" and eat.

CHILD CARRYING CHILD

When his [Jesus'] mother Mary had been engaged to
Joseph, but before they lived together, she was found to be
with child. Matthew 1:18

I'm pregnant
before the bridal bed,
can no longer hide

my protruding belly.
Disgraced at thirteen.
My parents walk

in shame. Knowing nods
as village women pass me,
whispers, sudden silences

at market as I reach
across the leeks
for fresh hard cucumbers,

sideways glances, teenage
friends avoid me, aghast
at the unwed mother.

How long
has this been going on?
My beloved Joseph, bags

under his eyes, will not look
at me. Archangel Gabriel is nowhere.
God does not protect me.

OUTSIDE THE ORDINARY

*God has been murdered. . . . The Master has been treated
in an unseemly fashion, his naked body not even deemed
worthy of a covering that his [nakedness] might not be
seen.* Melito of Sardis (d. c. 190) On the Pasch, 96–97

I invoke Einstein.
Here time
slows down,
space expands.

How could we
in ordinary time
murder God?

How could we
in ordinary space
contain our shame
at the nakedness
we exposed?

How could we
in ordinary time
and space
accommodate the mystery
of this evil?

But even Einstein's
plumb line has an end.

How could we
not note
in our ordinary
block of now
that God's mercy
has no edge?

TWO COUNT

WAR AND PEACE

[Mary] gave birth to her firstborn son and wrapped him in bands of cloth, and laid him in a manger. Luke 2:7

He took our face, was pushed
from Mary's womb.
The angels chanted peace,
Herod's swords pounded on doors,
Joseph buried the placenta.
Born in blood to blood.

With him comes also violence.

THE NEWS THAT CAN'T BE TOLD

When the sabbath was past, Mary Magdalene, and Mary the mother of James, and Salome, bought spices, so that they might go and anoint him. Mark 16:1

While it was still night
we started toward the tomb

with spices and oil
to anoint our Rabbi's body.

Inside the tomb
we saw an angel sitting

clothed in garments blazing white
as though he had swallowed the sun.

Even if it defies all logic,
we were there beside him

standing in the center
of the sun. The angel said,

He is risen,
go, tell Peter!

Stupefied by fear
stupefied by rapture

we fled,
told Peter nothing.

THE POLITICS OF LOVE

Now Judas, who betrayed him, also knew the place, because
Jesus often met there with his disciples. John 18:2

No need for me to grope
along the garden wall as blind men do.
I've been here before but now I come
with a fresh hole in my heart

and a fresh-bought kiss upon my lips.
When I betray the man I love
I betray my identity. Still,
I cannot deny necessity.

I must cut the bonds, become un-chosen
so I can push aside debris
of my people's failed hopes—the Romans,
like ziggurats in Ur, remain,

their lances poised, their pockets full
of taxes gouged from those
who sup on cactus bread and nettle broth.
For bloodied money to jingle

in my purse priests bought my tender
peck upon the cheek among the olive trees.
—The bitterest gall of all,
he loves me still.

SARAI IN PHARAOH'S BEDROOM

When [Abram] was about to enter Egypt, he said to his
wife Sarai, "I know well that you are a woman beautiful
in appearance; and when the Egyptians see you, . . . they
will kill me, but they will let you live. . . . And the woman
was taken into Pharaoh's house. Genesis 12:11, 12, 15

Beware, I tell myself,
when Abram seeks thick grass
in Egypt to feed his flock.

I must pull the cypress pegs,
fold our tent, cross the threat
of Egypt's border.

Will a sturdy breeding she-goat
pass the Pharaoh's border guards
unmolested? To save his guts,

my Abram, fresh from speaking
with God, asks me to lie
to Pharaoh's face, *I'm his sister,*

as the Lord of Egypt escorts me
to his harem to drop a son.
Abram, unashamed, stands mute

as Moloch's statue. To save me,
God sends Pharaoh purple boils
in groin and armpit.

My man uses me; he uses me.

IT'S A MAN'S WORLD

The man seized his concubine, and put her out to them. They wantonly raped her, and abused her all through the night until the morning. Judges 19:25

When concubine Susanna went to the well,
peach trees dropped their blossoms,
old men ogled,
young men grew thirsty.

She traveled with Jared to Gibeah
where pious Uzzi gave them bread and bed.
As night descended
toughs battered on the door
demanding Uzzi give them Jared
to lie with them.

Uzzi pleaded,
My friends, do not act
so vilely against my guest.
Even mountains
hide their peaks in shame
at this outrage.
The man is my guest.

The thugs kept hammering.
Uzzi offered them his virgin daughter
but they wanted a man.
They resumed the pounding
till Jared opened the door
and forced Susanna out.

Gang-raped till dawn
she crawled to Uzzi's threshold.

There she died.

SARAH'S LIST

God said to Abraham, "As for Sarai . . ." Genesis 17:15

Listen to me, Lord. I have a list.
You said to Abraham:
Go, leave your fathers' graves! To me,
no word. You promised him,
toothless at ninety-nine, a son. A son
of ours? We laughed. Sixty years
you locked my womb and then
told Abraham you would unbolt it.
To me, no word. Would Abraham
bulge, shriek, spread his legs
across the birthing stool? Is he the eagle,
I the guttersnipe, that his lordship's
wedded spouse must overhear the news
hidden behind a tent flap?
Do I exaggerate? You turned your face
to this old woman only
to accuse me of a niggling lie. Note!
The single time you spoke to me.
Do I exaggerate? The promise,
tell me! Where's the seal? In the snip
off Abraham's foreskin, but no mark
upon my breasts. And who consulted me
when you bid him burn my son
on Mount Moriah? Still I exaggerate?
Why did your hand-picked Abraham
twice turn me over to the harem of kings?
Am I a cow in heat needing to be mounted?
Why did I not see light in your light?
Why did your truth not set me free?

COME INTO MY BEDROOM

Bring the food into the chamber, so that I may eat from your hand. 2 Samuel 13:10

Ammon, the Golden Stallion,
had a passion for his sister, Tamar.
He feigned a fever, asked King David
to let her come into his quarters
to tend his needs.

The princess pushed back her yellow veil,
kneaded wheat dough,
baked walnut cakes
while Ammon lounged on the side,
his leg across the arm of a chair,
bragging of Jebusite battles won,
joking of brother Absalom oiling his long hair
and preening in the mirror.

Ammon invited Tamar
to bring her cakes into his bedroom
where they could be more comfortable.
She drew near, offered hot cakes,
gently extended her hand
to feel his fevered brow
when he grabbed and mounted her.
She clawed and screamed.

After the walnut cakes had cooled
he despised Tamar as a slut,
threw her into Jaffa street,
bolted the door against her.

Absalom told her to weep
in her chambers,
say no word at court.

After the peach trees had blossomed twice
and no man would look at Tamar
Absalom invited all his brothers
to feast at Baal-hazor.

When Ammon, in his cups,
rose to make a toast
Absalom slashed him.
He died cradling his guts
in his hands.

EVERY PROMISE A FANG

[Abraham] bound his son Isaac. Genesis 22:9

"Listen. Fold your tents,
gather up your flocks, abandon
your fathers' graves. *Go,*
I will make you a numberless nation."

In our decay, I seventy-five, barren Sarah
sixty-five, hear your promise.
The son of our decay will be great
in an unnamed land. Good to your word

you brought us to the soil of famine.
Eighty-eight and counting: still no son,
but promises renewed in blood.
Every promise a poisoned tusk,

every pledge of land and flocks
wrapped in jeopardy. My life
unravels in angry waiting
for your dyspeptic will.

Ninety-nine is past and Sarah weeps.
Again the covenant's reissued,
signed in my mutilated member
—Puberty rites just before the grave?—

When I'm a hundred Sarah blossoms.
We titter in our lumpy bed as though
we'd found the cosmology of love.
I lay my ear upon her belly

to hear his beating heart.
No one in Ur of Chaldees,
has seen antiquity spreading
legs upon a birth stool.

Sarah bleeds, screams, curses Eve,
curses the heavens,
whelps a roaring beast
whose howl is heard beyond

Beer-sheba and the sands of Ur.
When the lad is ten I hear:
"Go to Mount Moriah
to burn your boy upon the mountain,

the son you love." Betrayal lurks
behind every word of honor,
every promise is a fang.
What about fidelity?

Promises thrice vowed, a snare?
Like a rug merchant, you stall,
postpone delivery, renegotiate.
And now again you haggle,

with Isaac's blood for barter.
Is there no end to testing,
no honor among the gods?
Woe to the chosen, to the elect.

I bind Isaac on the altar of Moriah,
but you stay my hand. We return
to Beer-sheba heavy with knowing
God. I wait,   wary.

SLEEPING WITH MY WOMAN'S SLAVE

Sarai said to Abram, "May the wrong done to me be on you!" Genesis 16:5

I was patting my camel's neck
as it farted contentedly
while drinking from the Tigris
when I heard you say *Go!*, decisive
as an arrow in the gut.
I'm to leave Haran
for some unmentioned nowhere,
where my seventy-five-year-old seed,
shriveled as acacia when the wadi's dry,
will sprout a sturdy son?

At sixty-five Sarai's womb's withered,
her breasts sag
like decaying gourds.

For decades you yawn,
pick at the scab
on your left elbow,
dither with your hoe
in the cactus garden.

Thinking I'm asleep Sarai weeps her gall
into the pillow. At sunrise
she suggests God is not reliable,
not really;
says I should plow Hagar's garden.

Sarai unrolls my sleeping carpet,
lays the eager Hagar down
and calls me in.

When the slave blossoms
tears and accusations.

So now it's my fault.

SEVEN CARD STUD

Whoever believes in the Son has eternal life. John 3:36

Bluffing at poker with a pair
of deuces signifies I'm prepared to die.
Yet the game's not a Greek tragedy

where I bid against the fates
and know for sure I'll lose.
Nor will Zeus descend

Olympus to kill the wounded
who lost the last hand.
Still, I have four kings,

the pot heaps with $20 bills,
and lose to a Royal Flush.
But God's poker game's different.

I hold four aces
and a wild card and fold
because the Dealer has given me

a free pass to the Platinum Room
upstairs where pots are full
of $500 bills
and anyone can win.

I'VE BEEN THERE AND BACK

They gave a dinner for him [Jesus]. . . . Lazarus was one of those at the table with him. . . . It was on account of him [Lazarus] that many of the Jews were deserting and were believing in Jesus. John 12:2, 11

Sheol's the cave of ashes
and black mist, where even worms
are dead. No one returns,
but I've been there and back.

A crowd of Jews say they've come
to Bethany to dine with Jesus,
who named and called me
from the tomb. In truth,

they also want to see me,
the one who does not smell of death
but of burial spices
the way the sandal tree has no fragrance

until its felled. They call me friend
and grasp my arm, watch me drink the Syrian wine
and in between the toasts they pose
questions about what goes on up there.

Does Moses bend back and forth
when he reads Torah up there
so God will notice him? We know
there's no outside of God

but did you see his face?
You who have tasted eternal life
and found it sweet, will you taste death
again and find it bitter?

JACOB'S GOD ON PROBATION

If God will . . . give me bread to eat and clothing to wear
. . . then the LORD shall be my God. Genesis 28:20

Some things I cannot choose,
father, clan, and height.

But I will decide whether
I'll take Isaac's God as mine.

God should remember,
a promise is a promise. No diddling five

and twenty years before delivering
as with Abraham.

I'll not allow endless repetitions
of thin-worn pledges. No more

absurdities like asking Abraham
to sacrifice his only son.

If God delivers upfront,
I'll think about bending the knee

before him. Promises are not legal tender
and I lay down the terms.

If his angels bring fresh-baked bread,
supply five white mantles of lamb's wool,

if they find me a sturdy wife,
who makes my knees go weak,

then I'll consider bending the knee
before Isaac's God.

NOT A DAY OF SMALL THINGS

[Pilate] asked him, "Are you the King of the Jews?" Jesus said, "You say so." [Pilate asked him about the accusations.] But he gave him no answer. Matthew 27:11, 14

The Galilean stands like a sheep waiting
for the knife across the throat. To my questions,

nothing. No answer to the priests
—smelling of stale incense and treachery—

who want no trial, just the verdict.
Rather trust the Carthaginian thug caught

climbing out the treasury window
than the priests who lie for God.

The holy keepers of the Holy want him dead
and whipping will not do? Where's that basin of water?

NO VACATIONS

Keep awake therefore, for you know neither the day nor the hour. Matthew 25:13

If only vacations from God
      were possible
as when I burn my belly
      on Maui sands, two nights in Vegas,

fish three days outside of Missoula—
      all on company time. Damn
this God thing is unrelenting.
      I'm an honest man, but stealing

that arrogant pro's nine iron
      can't really be all that bad.
My boss goes on and on
      about my high maintenance

but the four martinis I drank
      alone at the bar were work-related
damage control.
      And the extra days in the Bahamas

were to grease a contract which still
      fell through. When pressed I lie,
but God elbows me and I lie again.
      Everywhere elbows.

GOD HAS NO IMAGINATION

The Israelites ate manna forty years. Exodus 16:35

God sends down the same old manna every day:
We make manna porridge, boiled manna,
baked manna, manna bread, fried manna,
and manna shepherd's pie.

Forty years of manna!

We detest this bread from heaven.

We *remember Egypt and the fish we took*
from the sea. We think of the cucumbers,
the melons, the leeks, the onions, and the cloves
of garlic. If only we had lamb chops and goat stew
—or even camels' humps
so tough one could not eat
unless boiled three days.

Our mothers' breasts go dry
as desert sands.

Why, like our oxen,
must we lick the morning dew from rocks?

God allows scorpions to creep
under our camel-skin blankets to avoid the cold.

Why did God bring us here to die?

CELIBATE AT TWENTY-FIVE

I remember one September evening when Joseph was alive
sitting together outside on our three-legged stools.
Quiet except for the baby crying next door.
Mary, I know he never drinks too much
and it's not that late. Anyway why should a man

of twenty-five always be at home
with dull parents. He's not a child.
After God dropped him
in our laps, breaking birth laws
as casually as bending Deuteronomy's decree

against boiling a kid in its mother's milk,
after all the dazzle at the beginning: angels singing,
shepherds kneeling, magi following a wandering star,
after all that—nothing, just nothing.
Doesn't make sense. You always say

that after the wondrous beginning
he's ordinary. Celibate at twenty-five!
That's ordinary? All his buddies have had children
since they were fifteen while he sleeps alone.
What about the obligation to marry?

Obviously likes women but the villagers have doubts.
I've seen wonder in his eyes in the presence
of the radiant Naomi, Moshe's radiant daughter.
I remember when we carried the bench
to Moshe's house and stopped to ask

Naomi about her father's health.
As the three of us continued down the hill
she pretended to stumble on a stone.
Jesus dropped his end of the bench, was at her side
with indecent haste, all smiles and charm—

But no—as though she were a gilded witch.

IT'S A TOUGH SELL

We proclaim Christ crucified. 1 Corinthians 1:23

I'm commissioned
to preach a failed messiah
and dead Savior. Might as well
pour priceless wine into the Nile.
Everyone who knows him,
his family too,
cannot imagine him a redeemer.
Some think him crazy.

This cabinet maker,
famed not for his cabinets
but for being the sole man in Nazareth
wifeless and sonless at thirty.

He speaks a cactus wisdom
yet chose twelve simpletons
needing baths and spines
who, like children,
abandon him when guards
rattle their swords. After

incensing the holy of holies
the priests gave him to the Romans.
Convicted of sedition, flogged,
paraded bleeding through the streets,

stripped, crucified, genitals publicly
displayed, racked
between Jerusalem's dregs.

Scum as messiah—a tough sell.

ALIMONY AND THE KINGDOM OF GOD

If you love me, you will keep my commandments. John 14:15

When I say *I love you*,
next comes feeding bums on skid-row,
ladling soup at Friendship House,
smiling at the ugly doorman.

No more dumping garbage on the highway,
or stealing bottles of gin from the club,
or cheating on my tax returns.

Could we do away with alimony?

Always obligations.
Why must I open a vein?
You'd think God would be different,

giving with no thought of a return.
God eats only when invited out, no grocery bills.
God's roof does not leak; no carpenter to pay.

God never needs a hip replacement.
No teeth that need a root-canal.
Why does it cost to love the Holy One?

COUNT THREE

A DIFFERENT KIND OF KNOWING

We speak God's wisdom, secret and hidden. 1 Corinthians 2:7

Nothing your eyes can see,
your fingers touch, your hand
grasp will tell you who

I am, but when the soldiers
lift me up, then you'll
know *I AM WHO AM.*

ON MY HONOR

If a shepherd has a hundred sheep, and one of them has gone astray . . . Matthew 18:12

Lord, this time will be different.
No tax fraud,
no savaging the boss behind her back.

I'll quit being an Ostrogoth, throwing away
underlings like yesterday's
Wall Street Journal.

I will swear off Vegas blackjack.
Lord, my hand upon my mother's casket,
no more demonizing the moron

who stole the sales I almost closed.
I'm finished staggering sideways
down the street with buddies (belts running

out of notches); finished weeping,
hugging the barman, cursing
every belligerent bastard.

Liver shot, detox thrice,
detectives tail the girlfriend, wife gone.
Lord, this time will be different.
Somewhere there's got to be meaning.

SARAI'S BRAG

Now Sarai, Abram's wife, bore him no children. Genesis 16:1

I'm fair Sarai, freeborn Sarai,
lawful wife, loved by pharaohs,
kings, and desert sheiks,
whom the man of faith from Ur

in Chaldees (he speaks to God,
but sleeps with me) twice stamped
as sex-passport into lands and beds
of foreign lords. My man wants me

to swear, "I'm not his wife." Thus
one passes on a prized and branded cow!
I'm no Hagar slave called under
goat-skins to warm Abram's nights

and pleasure him. No! I'm Sarai,
temple without an altar, who weeps
and asks if she is loved. Womb empty,
breasts dry. No son—no honor

no male baby—no incense.
I give my Hagar slave to lie with him,
who bears a son unto my knees,
but Adonai, Lord of Lords, says *No.*

So the seed of Abram is not enough.
I have my bragging rights.
Only I am loved by Abram.
Only I can bear the son of promise.

I'm Sarai, Mother of the Nation.

THE QUEEN LEANS OUT
THE PALACE WINDOW

David danced before the LORD with all his might. Michal
daughter of Saul looked out of the window. 2 Samuel 6:14, 16

For the hand of Michal I cut the foreskins
of a hundred Philistine men in arms and thought the price
too low. And this before I scarcely grew a beard.

Now my Queen leans out the palace window
as I process below. Every six steps
I sacrifice an ox, and dance like a mad Hittite

before the Ark of God mounting to Jerusalem
where the Lord will dwell among us in a tent.
I step right, step left, hop, strike the tambourine,

skip a beat to syncopate the rhythm,
while my mantle blows high to expose my manhood.
Michal rebukes me to my face as the village idiot

because I dance like a temple prostitute before the scum
of all Jerusalem. But God has chosen me
and I chose God. Before him I humble myself.

"Remember Michal, daughter of Saul,
I have seven other wives, ten concubines,
so my bed's never cold. Clasp the memory

of my warm chest against your breasts.
Never more will you slip
beneath the goat-skin blanket you made for me."

THE WHOLE PRIESTLY TRUTH

I'm chosen,
God's anointed
who knows shameless secrets.
Others slouch, stumble

on their shoestrings,
while I walk like a soldier
on parade, shoulders back.
I'm a torch lighting up

bat-infested caves,
sailors' pick-up dives.
I hold the keys to unlock
—or lock—

the stabbings in Dinky Town.
Besides, I know
where the bread is kept,
and how to slice it.

But I'm a bat
in my own cave
where I hang upside down,
smell my droppings.

FROM THE TRIBE OF IRRITABLE PROPHETS

Robert Bilheimer, 1917–2006, Pastor and Ecumenist

He always lived on the last
day of December, robbing
today's bank

to build tomorrow's skyscraper.
Gucci liked his suit and tie,
ready to be prof

in Dale Carnegie's Fifth Avenue
Charm School. A battering ram
against churches of Faith,

Hope, and Cadillacs,
a testy prophet, a hornets' nest
hounding his not-too-smart flock

up Mount Tabor's steep incline.
He refused to don a bathing suit
and lounge on Bahamas's beaches.

He wanted to build Bethlehem's
manger in Times Square
and call all the wise men

to bring gold for the breadless
and roofless. When he threw
gasoline on burning cinders,

Dorothy doused the conflagration
with water she had kissed to honey.
Time began when God made light

and ended for the cranky prophet
when the dark blotted out the sun.

THE VIEW FROM BELOW

Then Jesus gave a loud cry and breathed his last. . . . Now
when the centurion, who stood facing him, saw that in this
way he breathed his last, he said, "Truly this was God's Son."
Mark 15:37, 39

Standing beneath the rabbi's cross,
I watch his blood drip. Today
I nailed two naked crooks,
one naked rebel. Dark

covers the land like the black anger
of the gods of war. Just before
the rabbi dies he howls as if Mars
himself were sawing bone.

I'm goy, an uncircumcised centurion
with notches on my spear, who despises
Jews and Jewish squabbles that brought him
to this hill. When my spear pierces his

side blood and water splatter
on my head and breast.
Through bloody eyes I look up at him.
Now this goy knows.

BRUTUS AT CALVARY

Then all the disciples deserted him and fled. Matthew 26:56

I'm Matthew,
tax collector,
coward.
But now I'm brave
and write the truth.

Back then, like the others,
I turned my back
and with them
ran down the mount
with a sackfull

of reasons. Luke
finds my version
of the truth too raw,
cooks the story
for tender souls;
"acquaintances
and women stood

at a distance."
The bloody truth:
we men betrayed him
to terror of the nails,
were nowhere near the hill,
while women stood fast.

We were more than friends.

Noble Brutus also had his reasons.

THE DEATH OF A MATHEMATICIAN

Florian Muggli, osb, Mathematician (1925–2010)

Diapered Alzheimer, tied to the wheelchair,
corridor your sandbox, smooth brown
handrail leading nowhere, groping

for the edge of the real, slumped
into the long emptiness. I stand
in freedom, watch you stretch a palsied

hand, stroke shiny knobs,
open doors to your antiseptic dark
that covers the math of limits

and the infinite. The study of functions
to lift a rocket, gauge
the arc to the moon, ends

when your spoon cannot
calculate the distance from carrots
on the plate to your mouth.

THE JAPANESE RYOAN-JI DRY GARDEN
Kyoto, April 15, 1987

Purgatory-pure sand,
raked lines
like frozen ripples.
Six scabby
stand-alone rocks,
Sphinxes with nothing
to do but be,

calligraphy of the undivided.
In the corner
a pine, the solitary witness
to the possibility of dying.
Not a strolling garden

so I sat at the moss-axis
of the universe,
listened to the stones whisper
to the sand. They spoke
not of cold death
but of the density of life.
What is seen is not exactly
all there is.

I left by the path
near the stone
lantern which did not
light the way.

ANGRY BALLAD OF DEATH ROW WEST

Precious in the sight of the LORD is the death of his faithful
ones. Psalm 116:15

Ninety, with time for piety and pills,
I, Henry, am damn mad
and I intend to be difficult.

Potty trained by angels,
on good days I do not wet my pants.
I eat pabulum, watch Jeopardy,

dream of walking unassisted
down the hall. Intake hoses,
outtake hoses, sugar water

in the arm, drop by drop,
bitter pledge of the ersatz life.
Uriah swears he will drink hemlock,

pee blood, if one more children's choir
serenades defenseless monks.
They carried out poor Ivan who pushed

away the cottage cheese, turned his face
against the wall. Nurses of joy
gave dotty Kilian the wonder drug,

promising the skies, and, O, did it deliver.
Louis the Pious, whose forty ills are not enough,
stands at the door in scapular and collar,

Is it time for church?
The Abbot shouts salvation
in Jacob's ear (hearing aid turned off).

Harold, thrice broke his hip, will not go.
Whoever says life's fragile has never lived
on Death Row West. Nurses ask

about bowel movements, how big,
firm or soft. Freshly diapered
we stumble toward our God.

JOB SUES GOD

JOB, SALT, GOD

I summoned him to court. Job 9:16

God damn the day I was born!
Did my mother shriek, howl,
muscle this clump from the womb?

You say, *"Let there be darkness!"*
and sullen night dawned.
The first day.

It's not the dark prince
who's destroying me, but you.

You festered my sores.
I'd rather trust a Philistine sheep thief
with my camel
than the one who tears away my scabs,
pours hot salt upon my wounds.

I knock upon your door
to say, Let's talk about
my seven dead Goliath sons,
three dead Deborah daughters
of uncut hair.

You pretend you're out,
but I know you're in there.
You want me to think
you've withdrawn
into your eternity-cave.

When you slip out
I place my hand
upon your shoulder,
slap the summons in your palm,
call you into court.

You drop boulders
from your transcendental balcony,
put Satan's acid
in my arteries,
wound me on a whim,
yawn at my accusations.

No answer to my charges,
but you yammer on
about my sins.

I swear you're guilty
as I place my hand between my thighs.

BOASTS AND BANALITIES

You say, 'I am in the right before God.' Job 35:2

Some things only friends will tell you.
Your self-sufficient justice's
a lonely pyramid
because you refuse
to stand naked
in the holiness of God.
Don't make yourself important

by doubting God. You complain
about the absence of the Lord;
can you endure God's presence?
Because you've read one scroll
you instruct the Lord on how
to make the water blue? Do you sit

beside the Lord, whisper wisdom
in Wisdom's ear? You wrap banalities
in silk as though they're Torah,
build slingshot towers,
to throw blasphemies
at your God. As though
you're god himself you boast
of your rectitude, parade it
like a trophy.

Do you think God's a hen
who lays an egg, cackles
and sashays around the pen?

Grow up!

NOBLE LIES

[Job's three friends] met together to go and console and comfort him. Job 2:11

Friends, I do not stand in court
to negotiate with God.
You defend God dishonestly
even as he rolls loaded dice

upon the bench. You lounge
beneath a Juniper tree
because you think
its leaves reveal God's mysteries.
You tell noble lies
and say they're Torah.

As the code of Moses says
the Lord neither rewards robbers
nor scourges saints.

But consider the bandits who drink
from alabaster cups,
leprous fingers of the upright merchant.

You speak from old wisdom,
I from new pain.

Why do you,
dear friends, chisel my name
on Sheol's door to despair?

My conscience is not moldy flat-bread
I feed to dogs.

My doxologies are pure.

GOD ON THE DOCK

I will defend my ways to his face. Job 13:15

You're in court, Lord. Why
            cover your mask with your hands?
This is not a Greek tragedy where
            one can hide in rhetoric and still
strut off the stage in glory.

Am I a child that I must throw a tantrum
            before you notice I exist?
Before my accusations echo from the canyons
            you withdraw into clouds of temple incense.
Your credibility's a sieve; your promises

are mists on the mountains which vanish
            when the sun rises. When I seek your face
you hide behind your door of glory.
            Why lay snares for one who lies
at your feet? When my camel's winning

you move the goal line. You stalk
            as silent as a spider climbs its web.
You're a battering ram,
            though my gates decay, my walls are thin.
You change the rules, take no prisoners.

When we wrestle through the night
            and I'm winning, you cheat
as any thug from Askelon would do
            un-socketing my hip.
I limp away.

HARD QUESTIONS

Have the gates of death been revealed to you? Job 38:17

When I refused to meet you
outside the court, Job,
was it because I trembled
at your blasphemies?

You accuse me of absence
yet I hear you
vilify me. Who are you

to sue me?
Do volcanoes vomit
when you pass?
Can you measure the sea
pot by pot?
Do you tilt the clouds
for rain? Do you sing
with stars for notes?
So the sun rises

from your tent?
Did you give the camel
two sets of eyelids,
create the dromedary
so it can close its nostrils
in sand storms?
Did you create female goats
with beards?
You, Job, created all this?

Tell the court!

LET ME FLUFF THE PILLOW

[Job said] . . . My justice was like a robe and a turban.
Job 29:14

Like all seducers, Lord, you despise
the one you led to the bed.

In former days you secured the tent flap
against me. Why? All I wanted
was to sit beside you,
dip my bread into your cup.

Your justice is the cloak
you threw off when you
cast your clothes upon the floor.

Did my unsullied life
carry within it
the condemnation of yourself?
Did you test me to see
if I'd serve for nothing?

Lord, you spoke soft words,
led me to the bed,
seduced me in the evening,
left me in the morning.

ON THE HIGHEST ZIGGURAT

Now my eye sees you. Job 42:5

Forgive me, Lord.
I spoke of things
I could not know.
If I climbed the highest ziggurat,
I could not touch
your lowest mystery.

My friends have lied for you,
hung a goat bell
around my innocence.
Still I hear the footsteps
of your mercy running
toward me.

You've removed scales
from my eyes.
Now no icon
between me
and the skin
of your face

I touch.
I hear you call my name
You take me
by the hand,
lead me to your tent,
sit me at your table,
serve me wine
you pressed.

I engrave your name
upon my tongue.

RIGGING THE MYSTERIES

The LORD said to Eliphaz the Temanite: "My wrath is kindled against you and against your two friends; for you have not spoken of me what is right, as my servant Job has. Job 42:7

So you're the friends
who stripped the flesh
from Job's bones,
defended me dishonestly,
rigged my mysteries. You sat

upon my cosmic throne,
rattling my quiver
as though I were eager
to war, impatient
with the man
who longed for me
even as he placed a foot
upon the boundaries
of blasphemy.

Your lies are failed truths.
I've healed Job's lacerations,
given back more sheep

than folds can hold.
My wrath sweeps you
into prison where Job,
your accommodating jailer,
plays your advocate.
Even now
beyond the bars
he bends his knees, weeps
and prays for you.

I engrave Job's name
upon my tongue.

NOTES ON THE POEMS

Page 15. "Hammer, Spike, Mary." The words of Jesus at the wedding feast in Cana when he momentarily refused Mary's implied request for help cannot escape from "some element of harshness" (John J. Maloney, *The Gospel of John* [Collegeville, MN: Liturgical Press, 1998], 71). After Jesus began his ministry, "he left Nazareth and made his home in Capernaum by the sea" (Matt 4:13; see also Mark 2:1), where Peter lived. The house of Simon Peter and his brother Andrew is mentioned so many times in the gospels that sometimes it is simply referred to as "his [Peter's] house." On one occasion Jesus was already there when Peter returned from Galilee (Matt 17:25). The remains of the house were uncovered in 1968.

Page 70. "Job, Salt, God." Swearing by one's testicles is a practice rooted in the history of ancient Rome (but not in Greek antiquity) and in the early history of Israel. See Abraham, Genesis 24:2; Isaac, Genesis 47:29. The translation of the opening sentence is taken from Steven Mitchell's *The Book of Job* (New York: HarperCollins, 2002).